Manuel Knaus

Macro economic issues of offshore outsourcing

Manuel Knaus

Macro economic issues of offshore outsourcing

GRIN Verlag

Bibliografische Information der Deutschen Nationalbibliothek: Die Deutsche Bibliothek verzeichnet diese Publikation in der Deutschen Nationalbibliografie; detaillierte bibliografische Daten sind im Internet über http://dnb.d-nb.de/ abrufbar.

1. Auflage 2004
Copyright © 2004 GRIN Verlag
http://www.grin.com/
Druck und Bindung: Books on Demand GmbH, Norderstedt Germany
ISBN 978-3-638-65140-0

Macro economic issues of offshore outsourcing

- seminar paper -

Chair of Information Systems Management I
University of Mannheim

June 2004

by

Manuel Knaus

Filderstadt

Index

Figures

Glossary of Acronyms

DC	Developing country
EU	European Union
Fig	Figure
GDP	Gross Domestic Product
ICT	Information and Communication Technology
IT	Information Technology
MEEC	Middle and East European Country
R&D	Research and Development
u.a.	Unknown author
u.l.	Unknown location
US	United States
USA	United States of America

Currencies:

€	Euro
US$	United States Dollar

Summary

Topic of this paper are the macro economic issues of offshore outsourcing.

First inland and offshore outsourcing are described, especially focused on IT outsourcing.

Then reasons for IT offshore outsourcing are illustrated. Popular offshore markets are introduced and the advantages are shown.

In the next chapter, problems and risks of offshore outsourcing are explained. Both the more general view and IT specific problems and risks are described. Here general problems as well as problems of IT outsourcing are mentioned.

Then consequences of the offshoring trend are illustrated. Apart from consequences for IT branch, especially consequences for national economies of western countries, e.g. Germany, are viewed in detail. There can be short term and long term consequences. Future offshore outsourcing trends help to understand the effects. The development of unemployment caused by offshoring is one main focus.
Furthermore offshoring trends in other white collar work besides IT are shortly described.

At the end this the paper develops an idea about possible solutions for western countries. Potential reactions of the government and suggestions on how to create new jobs are presented in detail.

The paper finally ends with a small conclusion.

1. Conceptual introduction

1.1 Outsourcing

Outsourcing is an invented word of "outside", "resource" and "using" and means the long term branching out of previously self done services to an external vendor (Allweyer, T., Besthorn, T. and Schaaf, J., 2004). This vendor will do the work for the company. "Classical" outsourcing takes place in the same country. In this case, the vendor often takes over employees of the outsourced section.

In former times outsourcing has taken place only in areas like canteen, supply and security, in the last 15 years outsourcing became popular in all major sections of a company like production, R&D, financial services, telecommunication and IT.

Outsourcing is done to realize saving potentials, to transfer fix costs into variable ones, to get a higher service level and to free resources and focus on core competencies and strategic goals (Pohl, A. and Onken, B. R., 2003). More details will follow.

Apart from to complete outsourcing, there are other ways of outsourcing.
"Outtasking" or "selective outsourcing" is the assigning of single and middle term oriented tasks to an external vendor.
"Multisourcing" or "multi-vendor-outsourcing" is a complete outsourcing not to a single vendor, but different tasks to different vendors (Söbbing, T., 2002).
Outtasking and multisourcing are not the main focus of this paper, therefore they will not be discussed in detail.

1.2 Outsourcing in offshore markets

When outsourcing doesn't take place with a vendor within the home country of the company, but with a vendor from a different country, outsourcing is called "offshore outsourcing", "offshoring" or "international outsourcing".
Popular offshore markets are in developing countries (DCs) like India, China, Vietnam and in Middle and East European Countries (MEECs). In these countries more and more vendors appear on the scene.

Opposite to inland outsourcing, tit is very unusual for the vendor to take over employees from the outsourcing company.

1.3 IT outsourcing

At IT outsourcing, own responsibilities of the IT department are given to an external vendor. The service level can reach from only advice to individual implementation and maintenance of hard- and software (Bräutigam, P., 2004) up to outsourcing of the complete IT department. Several services are often bundled in one outsourcing deal.

As Fig. 1 shows, most popular is outsourcing of programming individual software, but other tasks are gaining more popularity.

IT outsourcing is often connected to the use of newest technologies and processes by the vendor, which have not been used before by a company. This issue will be discussed in detail later.

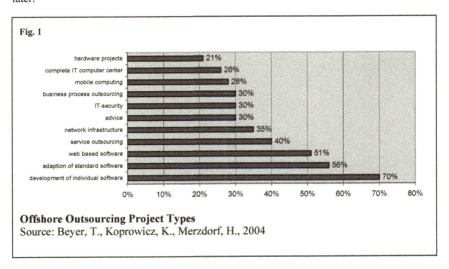

Fig. 1

Offshore Outsourcing Project Types
Source: Beyer, T., Koprowicz, K., Merzdorf, H., 2004

2. Reasons for offshore outsourcing

2.1 Advantages of offshore outsourcing

Obviously the most important reason for companies to outsource is to save money. Wages for IT personnel in DCs are much lower as in western countries. Experience shows, that cost

reductions of 25 up to 45% can be achieved through outsourcing (Parikh, M., Saranjit, A., 2002).

In a study 75% of managers said "considerable", when asked how big the cost advantage between Germany and MEECs is (Beyer, T. et. al, Fig. 8, 2004). But as Fig. 2 shows, the actual cost savings differ between the companies. Other expected benefits of offshoring, like better service quality, are mentioned here as well.

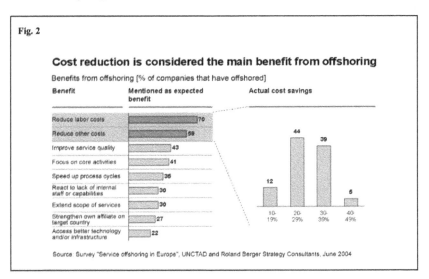

Fig. 2

Cost reduction is considered the main benefit from offshoring

Benefits from offshoring [% of companies that have offshored]

Source: Survey "Service offshoring in Europe", UNCTAD and Roland Berger Strategy Consultants, June 2004

Another point is the lack of high skilled personnel in western countries. Especially during the IT boom around 1997, in a number of countries within the EU, there where far to less IT people. The efforts of DCs to educate high qualified people now bears fruits and more and more DCs have very well trained IT personnel.

A further point is the possibility to adjust services or projects more flexible, depending on what the company needs. Also there is - especially contrary to Germany – more flexibility at daily and weekly working hours.

2.2 Facts of some developing countries

Looking at reasons and consequences of offshore outsourcing without analyzing the qualities of some popular offshoring countries is hardly possible. Therefore popular DCs are briefly described.

India

India is the most popular country for outsourcing. Also in daily press - especially in Germany - people can read about companies offshoring to India. Indian IT Specialists are in the view of German managers acknowledged, particularly since the federal government attracted these people to work in Germany with a work permit called "Green Card".

Following the U.S. American trend, India has become a popular offshore country also for European companies.

The turnover in the Indian IT sector has increased exponentially in the last years, from 2 Billion US$ in 1994 to 12.2 Billion US$ in 2001 (Singh, N. 2002). There are about 2500 vendors. 63% of them are serving U.S. markets and 26% European markets (Singh, N. 2002). One big advantage of India is, that most people speak English fluently (Schramm, J., 2004).

Bill Gates said about the Indian IT sector: „Three years ago India was emerging as an IT superpower. Today the country is handling most sophisticated projects in the world [...]. I am impressed with the talent we have in our India development center and the quality of the software being developed" (Pohl, A., Onken, B. R., 2003).

Vietnam

Vietnam, a socialist country in south east Asia, is one of the newer entrants in the IT offshoring business.

It has big industrial parks, where most of the IT companies reside (Chidamber, S.R., 2003).

Vietnam has reached a big economic growth in the last decade, 6.8% by 2001 (Statistisches Bundesamt, 2002), and its ICT Sector has gained a significant percentage of the economy growth (Chidamber, S.R., 2003).

Experts believe that the Vietnamese ICT sector has big growing potential and will play a increasing role for the economy (EU Counselors, 2003).

Russia

Russia is popular, because it has very good IT specialists. A world bank member said about the Russians: "Since the Russian education system continues to be heavily weighted towards math and science, Russian scientists are often considered the best in the world. Consequently, Russian IT companies present an attractive investment opportunity because these businesses

can draw upon Russia's large "intellectual resource" of world-class scientists and engineers" (Riabov, S., 2003).

Although the market, with about 4 billion US$ in 2002, is relatively small, it has a good growing potential. Especially the offshore centers in Moscow, St. Petersburg and Novosibirsk are well positioned in the market (Lekaeva, I., 2002).

China

The communistic China has become an important market for most western countries. There has been an impressive economic growth in the last years, always over 7 %, especially the service sector is growing rapidly (Statistisches Bundesamt, 2002).

China has discovered the potential of offshoring and is trying to enter the market with low price offers. The Chinese government has taken care of better education, especially IT education and has limited taxes. With the constructing of high-tech parks China want to attract foreign investors.

At the beginning of offshoring business, China has best chances to get assignments from Japanese companies, because it is compatible in culture, language and geographically in the vicinity (Zhonghua, Q., Brocklehurst, M., 2003).

Middle and East European countries

Especially for European countries like Germany, France or Great Britain MEECs are an attractive market for offshore outsourcing.

Poland, the Czech Republic, Slovakia, Hungary and others are smart locations for offshoring. As new entrants or close by the European Union, they are geographically nearby, politically stable, participate at the huge EU domestic market, profit from EU development funds, but have cheaper cost structures.

To participate at the IT outsourcing development, in the last years there arise several outsourcing firms in MEECs as well as big IT companies invested there (Allweyer, T. et al., 2004).

Consequently its interesting for companies to have a closer look on MEECs.

2.3 Excellence or inferiority of the offshoring services

Apart from cost savings, western countries have some omissions or problems due to they outsource.

Sometimes inside a company, especially at the IT department, there is a lack of innovation. Even if the companies try to update their services, often knowledge or state of the art technology is missing and there are time honored cost structures.

Possibly external vendors could deliver these services or technologies faster, more innovatively and have additional intelligence in the subject.

But do vendors have to be offshore or could they be inland outsourcers?

It could be criticized, that one problem of offshore outsourcing is the lack of quality. But it is not always certain, that the quality of services is better in western countries.

In matter of quality DCs have made progress, especially in the last years. Nowadays the majority of them have at least reached the status of western countries or are nearby to surpass western countries.

But there are a number of problems and barriers that limit them. These limits, outsourcing risks and also more details about offshore outsourcing will be shown next.

3. Problems with offshore outsourcing

We have seen many chances of outsourcing, but there are also several risks.

3.1 Risks and problems of outsourcing

Sometimes companies complain about a lack of control, for the reason that the vendor is geographically far away. They then have little chance to control and supervise him.

In opposite to the outsourcing company the vendor has more information about the outsourcing subject, e.g. cost structure. This leads to an information asymmetry, the so called "principal-agent problem" (Allweyer, T. et al., 2004). This is a general problem, also at inland outsourcing.

Another risk is the long term orientation of the contracts. This leads to financial and general dependence, because it mostly is not possible to change the vendor rapidly or to in-house the service again.

Another problem is the dissatisfaction of the employees of the company, because some of them are loosing their jobs or being transferred to other locations or departments. A number

of them even complain, that they have been forced to train foreign employees only to see their own jobs eliminated and their trainees sent back to their country of origin in order to help set up offshored operations (Schramm, J., 2004).

There are also hidden costs which can not be seen at first sight. These are transaction costs, contract managing costs, costs for selecting an offshore vendor, not correctly specified issues in the contract and many more (Lacity, M.C., Hirschheim., R., 1993).
Therefore solid calculations have to be done before signing the contract. Exact definitions of the outsourcing services have to be fixed, for example service level agreements.

3.2 Problems in developing countries
Although much effort, DCs have still major problems in various areas.

One problem is the possible failure of a vendor to deliver the services. This could happen especially with small vendors and in less developed countries. Multisourcing could be an option to reduce this risk.
Occasionally companies complain about a lock of abiding agreements. Because of dissimilar mentalities, people in DCs sometimes make agreements, even if they know the are not able to fulfil them (Brightman, I., 2004).
Sometimes a lack of legal security hinder western companies to make larger outsourcing contracts. The governments of DCs should support their own firms with this problem.

Also the political system and stability of foreign markets are leading to caution. This especially is the case at countries with political risks like terrorism, war, and other internal or external conflicts.

Most problems occur not only in DCs. They crop up through obstacles between DCs and western countries, which are described now.

3.3 Barriers between western and developing countries
There are factors that create barriers to offshore outsourcing between western and DCs.

In DCs there is in some areas only an underdeveloped or poorly developed ICT infrastructure (Narhar, N., Käkölä, T., Huda, N., 2002). This on the one hand leads to high communication costs, and on the other hand outsourcing there appears to be hard.

There are cultural differences which lead to various problems. One example is the lack of language skills, which leads to communication problems.
Especially communication through computer based media leads to problems. Not native English speaking people for example use many words differently, which leads to misunderstandings (Narhar, N. et al., 2002).

A further problem is security. Transferring data via networks, the protection of intellectual property and the risk of industrial espionage are leading to concerns (Allweyer, T. et al., 2004). This particularly is a problem, because national espionage programs, which many nations have, are following own security interests. Possibly there could be backdoor code or worms in software products (Hall, M., 2003). This can lead to big economic losses.

Time Zone differences could be an advantage for 24h R&D, but could also have disadvantages, e.g. when there are live interactions necessary. Flexible working hours are needed then (Brightman, I., 2004).

Especially in India these barriers are most far-reaching fallen down.

4. Consequences for western countries

4.1 Current and future IT outsourcing trends

Major Research Companies prognosticate an increase of IT outsourcing of 10-14% yearly (Bräutigam, P., 2004).
Fig. 3 shows the prognoses for the IT outsourcing market value in Europe and Germany for the next years.
Because of this, there is an enormous potential for vendors especially in DCs. They will increase there efforts to overcome the barriers to participate in the economic grow.

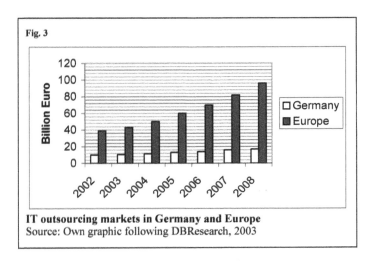

IT outsourcing markets in Germany and Europe
Source: Own graphic following DBResearch, 2003

Because of increasing competition, also from U.S. vendors like IBM that want to undercut Indian vendors, offshore prices will fall (Moore, S., 2003).

In offshore markets the number of mergers and acquisitions will increase (Moore, S., 2003). This will lead to a stronger market power of fewer vendors.

Problems in western countries, especially the increasing pressure to save costs, will result in outsourcing also critical IT components. Most medium and big size enterprises will increasingly think about outsourcing (Bräutigam, P., 2004).

"Classical" offshoring countries like India will get new competitors from countries with lower costs like China, Vietnam and Latin American countries. This will lead to stronger competition. Perlitz (2000) has called this phenomenon "international hunting line", shown in Fig. 4.

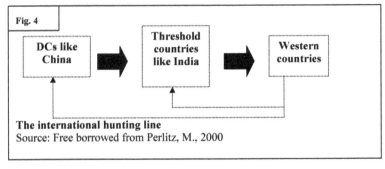

The international hunting line
Source: Free borrowed from Perlitz, M., 2000

While "hunting" countries have low costs, wages in India will grow. Indian vendors will have to climb up the value chain and offer more complete service solutions to maintain its position (Moore, S., 2003). At the same time, western countries have to keep up their leading in relation to "threshold countries" to survive. Possibilities to do so are shown later.

4.2 Consequences for the western IT branch

As the IT branch is one of the driving forces for German economy, getting problems there will result in problems for the whole economy (Pols, A., 2004).

On the one hand, because of the possibility to offshore, companies and also smaller firms are increasingly forced to think about offshore outsourcing, at least of parts of the IT, because their competitors may realize cost saving potentials. Therefore many specialists and advisors are needed.

On the other hand, IT vendors in western countries have to react on that threat. They could go into partnerships with vendors in DCs, they could do mergers or acquisitions, or they could built own subsidiaries in DCs.

On the other side they can try to differentiate their services from offshore vendors, for example through offering faster reaction times, more complete solutions, better security or better individual maintenance.

4.3 Consequences for the national economy of Germany

In 2003 about 6 % of the German GDP, about 129 billion €, was achieved in the ICT sector (Heil, I., Simon, P., 2004). As we have seen in Fig. 3, the market value of IT outsourcing in Germany is already high and will increase in the next years. This indicates, that this is a substantial part of the German economy.

Therefore it's important to achieve a win-win situation between both the outsourcing country like Germany and the offshore country.

One benefit can be, that because of the savings companies achieve through offshoring, additional reinvestments can be done. These reinvestments can bring further productivity and cost savings to the company, and new or secured working places and taxes for the economy (Schramm, J. 2004).

Another benefit is, that more prosperity in offshore countries will lead to more needs of high-tech and other products offered by German companies. This also leads to a higher revenues through more exports (Allweyer, T. et al., 2004).

Offshoring countries will get an increasing standard of living and a economic growth. Increasing wages of DCs will lead to a curbing of the rising of offshoring and thus to a stabilisation of the situation for both (Moore, S., 2003).

But there is also the possibility to get a lose-lose situation. This means, that the consumer spending in the outsourcing country get less because of higher unemployment and stagnating wages. This could get a negative impact on the productivity rate and the growth (Schramm, J., 2004). This again leads to lower request for offshore outsourcing services, and so offshore countries will get problems.

The third possibility is a lose-win situation. Here offshore countries get economic strength. They are able to do more and more offshoring also in different economic areas and get own competitive big companies.

And on the other side the German economy gets a regression because of the loose of competitiveness and the technological lead. This would result in many negative consequences for Germany.

Trade unions for example, which are strong in Germany, are very concerned about the offshoring trends especially in MEECs and will increase their efforts against it (Brinkley, I, 2004). More pressure of trade unions could hinder some of the outsourcing plans. This would have negative corollary for the companies.

It also is possible, that a number of companies, because of this fact, decide to leave Germany. In a greater degree, no economy is able to afford this.

4.4 Development of unemployment in western countries

If more and more high-skilled jobs in western countries go offshore, what are the consequences for the development of unemployment? Must academicians worry?

Especially in Germany and other EU countries unemployment is a big problem.

Fig. 5 shows the development of unemployment in Germany in the last years. With over 4 million unemployed people, a further increasing of the unemployment rate would have

negative repercussions for the German economy, the public finances and the social security system.

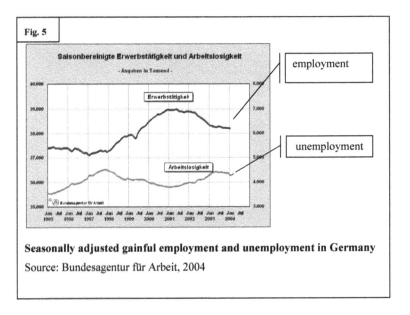

Seasonally adjusted gainful employment and unemployment in Germany
Source: Bundesagentur für Arbeit, 2004

Although in Germany there is less offshoring than in the US or Great Britain, Allweyer (2004) prognosis a loss of 50,000 employees in the IT sector until 2008 directly.

High unemployment has multiple reasons. One big problem are very high working costs in Germany in all working areas. Another point are exorbitant additional costs for the social security system paid for each employee.

Unemployment is still mainly a problem of blue collar work. But with increasing offshoring of white collar work this could change rapidly. The economy can not afford the loss of many high skilled working places.

But in the positive case, through a bigger growing of the economy because of offshoring, there could be a restrained effect to the unemployment.

Possible solutions to defend the unemployment resulted by offshoring are treated in chapter 5.

13

4.5 Crossover of the offshoring trend towards other economic areas

Because of enhanced technology, especially in the ICT sector, nowadays it is possible to offshore outsource easily also high skilled work. But not only in areas with main emphasis on IT, also in other economic areas there is an opportunity to offshore.

This could be outsourcing of health care services such as surgical operations, e.g. bypass surgery or angioplasty, or dental treatments (Zakariah A., 2004). These are mostly standardized services with luxury nursing.

What today is called medical tourism, that means that people privately go to DCs like India to be operated there, will in the future intensify. Increasingly health insurances will pay this, because they are not willingly or able to pay the strongly increasing medical prices in the home country. The costs, including flight and hotel, are between one half and one fifth of costs in western countries (Zakariah A., 2004).

This could result in a new offshore outsourcing segment, a progress which marks a higher level in the offshore outsourcing development and have to be viewed carefully.

5. Possible solutions

5.1 Creation of new jobs

To survive, Germany must constantly create new and innovative ideas and try to remain on the top of new innovative areas of research like nanotechnology, biotechnology, fuel cell technology or others. These trends have to be recognized early by research, business an the government and have to be supported.

Also public and business have to intensify their connections at basic research in major areas.

High skilled jobs that have been outsourced can be replaced by jobs in new areas. Allweyer (2004) called this process refining of the production.

In addition, within the EU, bigger research projects can be financed and cross border information exchange can help gaining a competitive advantage.

14

However, in the long term development, this means the time after 2020, we don't have to worry about a high unemployment. Because of the demographic development, fewer people and owing to more persons over 70 especially fewer employees will remain (Birg, H., 2004). The unemployment rate will sink massively. Thus negative trends from the outsourcing can be compensated.

In addition offshoring could, in the optimistic case, help compensating a probable lack of qualified employees in the future (Birg, H., 2004).

5.2 Adjusting screw of macroeconomic parameters

In spite of many not controllable influences there are many possibilities for western governments and the economy to take influence on the future effected by offshoring. There can be early actions, if problems or chances are discovered before time, or late reactions, if something goes wrong.

One step would be to support the building and extension of economic clusters. There, many high tech enterprises work in the same area under best conditions like modern infrastructure, nearby universities, good supply firms and others. Examples where this have already be done in Germany are the chip production nearby Dresden, called "Micropolis", and the high tech center around Munich (Solbrig, K., 2003). In the IT sector inland outsourcers so could give companies better service.

More investments in infrastructure, especially in modern ICT infrastructure, can help holding the lead compared to DCs.

In international comparison, with investments in knowledge of 4.7 % of the GDP in 2000, Germany is only in the middle. The USA with 6.8 % are leading.

Besides Germany has only the half amount of highly qualified graduates (Heil, I., Simon, P., 2004). For that reason another aim should be more investments in research and development as much as in education. This would be an early setting of the course for future success.

Labour costs in Germany have to sink, at least to the level of other leading high tech nations. Especially at costs for the social security system there is a need for action.

More flexible working conditions and relaxed restrictions would also be of assistance there.

15

To support the national economy, the Government can advance their efforts to achieve international agreements to protect the national companies. This can be for example in areas like industrial espionage, the protection of intellectual property or the legal security. Otherwise companies will get disadvantages.

But to much excessive desire for actions of the government could result in negative impacts. Economic shielding through penalty duties, trade barriers, shielding or travelling restrictions can have opposite results. Moreover legal restrictions of offshore outsourcing would not lead to positive effects.

Also if the Government tries to reduce taxes and fees in a massive amount, trying to compete with DCs, the economy will get big problems, without obtaining the hoped effect.

5.3 Future of offshore outsourcing

In economy there have been many trends, which were "modern" only a time period. The query is now, will the offshore outsourcing trend continue, or is it a temporal development and will decrease in the next decade?

As we have seen, because the offshoring trends is dynamically, climbing up the ladder from blue collar to white collar work, and from there constantly into more complex regions, it seems, that offshoring will have a longer future.

As long as there are major differences in costs, stable political environments and other factors between DCs and western countries are remaining favorable for offshoring, it will stays an interesting option for companies (Schramm, J., 2004).

6. Conclusion

As shown, consequences through offshore outsourcing for national economies of western countries can not be avoided. Job losses will come. An increasing of offshoring, also in different areas of high skilled work, is only a matter of time. More and more DCs will struggle to get offshoring services. Leading offshoring countries will present more complex service solutions with best quality.

The question is, can the economy cope with it? Can the economy handle this challenge? Is it able to profit from this development? Can this lead to more prosperity of western countries? The adjusting screws can be turned now.

16

Whereas companies should consider offshore outsourcing only after careful considerations, western governments should recognize the problems, think about them and act if necessary.

Getting a positive environment for business, helping to create jobs in new innovative areas of research, investing strongly in education and training of people, can help avoiding negative effects.

So hopefully both western and developing countries can profit from offshore outsourcing.

VI

Bibliography

Allweyer, T., Besthorn, T. and Schaaf, J.: *IT outsourcing: between starvation diet and nouvelle cuisine*, Deutsche Bank Research, Frankfurt am Main, 2004 http://www.dbresearch.de/PROD/DBR_INTERNET_DE PROD/ PROD0000000000078395.pdf (2004-05-03).

Beyer, T., Koprowicz, K., Merzdorf, H.: *Auslagerung von IT-Dienstleistungen nach Mittel- und Osteuropa*, Skilldeal AG, Berlin, 2004 http://www.sibb.de/Downloads/skilldeal_OffshoreStudie2_Ergebnisse.pdf (2004-03-07).

Birg, H.: *Bevölkerungsentwicklung*, Informationen zur politischen Bildung Nr. 282, Bundeszentrale zur politischen Bildung, Bonn, 2004.

Bräutigam, P.: *IT-Outsourcing: Eine Darstellung aus rechtlicher, technischer und vertraglicher Sicht*, Erich Schmidt Verlag GmbH & Co., Berlin, 2004.

Brightman, I.: *Making the off-shore call: The road map for communications operators*, Deloitte Touche Tohmatsu, London, 2004 http://www.deloitte.com/dtt/cda/doc/content/Deloitte%20Research_Offshoring%20Call_Mar2004.pdf (2004-07-06).

Brinkley, I.: *Global Offshoring*, TUC, London, 2004 http://www.tuc.org.uk/economy/tuc-7732-f0.cfm (2004-05-03).

Bundesagentur für Arbeit, *Saisonbereinigte Erwerbstätigkeit und Arbeitslosigkeit*, Nürnberg, 2004 http://www.pub.arbeitsamt.de/hst/services/statistik/000000/html/start/gif/et_alo.gif (2004-04-26).

Chidamber, S.R.: *A Analysis of Vietnam's ICT and Software Services Sector*, Kogod School of Business, American University, Washington D.C., 2003 http://www.is.cityu.edu.hk/research/ejisdc/vol13/v13r9.pdf (2004-03-08).

EU Counselors, u.a., *EU economic and commercial counselors 2003 report*, Hanoi, 2003 http://www.germanembhanoi.org.vn/de/wirtschaft/vn_wirtschaft/eu-report.pdf (2004-06-21).

Hall, M.: *Security risk associated with the new Outsourcing model – The Offshore Outsourcing Explosion*, KPMG, u.l., 2003 http://isacahouston.org/html/meetings_files/ISACA%20Presentation%20Outsourcing %20Risks1.pdf (2004-10-05).

Heil, I., Simon, P.: *Deutschland in Zahlen*, Institut der deutschen Wirtschaft, Deutscher Instituts-Verlag GmbH, Köln, 2004.

Lacity, M.C., Hirschheim., R.: *Information Systems Outsourcing: Myths, Metaphors and*

VII

Realities, John Wiley & Sons Ltd, Baffins Lane a.o., 1993.

Lakaeva, I.: *Trends in the Russian IT Market*, U.S. Commercial Service, Moscow, 2002
http://www.outsourcing-russia.com/kb/docs/russia/r08072-02.pdf (2004-05-25).

Moore, S.: *IT Trends 2004:Offshore Outsourcing*, Giga Research, u.l., 2003
http://www.satyam.com/homenews/documents/it2004_giga.pdf (2004-04-20).

Narhar, N., Käkölä, T., Huda, N.: *Software Production in Developing and Emerging Countries through International Outsourcing*, University of Jyväskylä, Finland, Jyväskylä, 2002
www.cc.jyu.fi/~naznaha/Outsourcing2.pdf (2004-03-06).

Parikh, M., Saranjit, A.: *Outsourcing Software Development*, Milan Associates, New Malden, 2002
http://www.milanassociates.com/pdf/OutsourcingWhitePaper.pdf (2004-05-10).

Perlitz, M.: *Internationales Management*, 4th edition, Lucius und Lucius, Stuttgart, 2000.

Pohl, A. and Onken, B. R.: *Outsourcing und Offshoring mit indischen IT-Unternehmen. Die IT Welt im Wandel*, Deloitte & Tauche, München, 2003
http://www.deloitte.com/dtt/article/Outsourcing und Offshoring mit indischen IT-Unternehmen.pdf (2004-03-06).

Pols, A.: *Daten zur Informationsgesellschaft: Status quo und Perspektiven Deutschlands im internationalen Vergleich*, Bitkom, Berlin, 2004
http://www.bitkom.org/gbgateinvoker.cfm/BITKOM_Daten_zur_Informationsgesellsc haft_2004.pdf (2004-04-20).

Riabov, S.: *IT Outsourcing for German High Tech Companies: Gaining Competitive Advantages in the Global Economy*, Auriga Inc., u.l., 2003
http://www.auriga.com/company/Rus_Germ_IT_Forum_Cebit2003.pdf (2004-05-10).

Schramm, J.: *Workplace Visions No.2: Offshoring*, SHRM Research, Alexandria, VA, 2004
http://www.shrm.org/trends/visions/2issue2004/0402WorkpcVisions.pdf (2004-05-03).

Singh, N.: *India's Information Technology Sector*, University of California , Santa Cruz, 2002
http://www.oecd.org/dataoecd/30/2/2399797.ppt (2004-04-26).

Söbbing, T., *Handbuch IT Outsourcing: Rechtliche, strategische und steuerliche Fragen*, mitp-Verlag, Bonn, 2002.

Solbrig, K.: *Chip, Chip, hurra: Dresden kommt*, Sächsische Zeitung, Dresden, 2003-03-25.

Statistisches Bundesamt Deutschland, Wiesbaden, 2002
http://www.destatis.de/cgi-bin/ausland_suche.pl (2004-03-17)
http://www.destatis.de/download/d/veroe/laenderprofile/lp_china.pdf (2004-03-17).

Zakariah A., Indian Healthcare Federation, New Delhi, 2004

http://www.indianhealthcarefederation.org/pressroom.html (2004-06-14).

Zhonghua, Q., Brocklehurst, M.: *What will it take for China to become a competitive force in offshore outsourcing?*, Journal of Information Technology 18, Page 53–67, London, 2003.

www.ingramcontent.com/pod-product-compliance
Lightning Source LLC
LaVergne TN
LVHW042258060326
832902LV00009B/1127